Gathering

Poems
Jackene Laverty

Illustrations
Karen Light

For:

Sunitha Narayanan

who made the connection
that led to this collaboration

Contents

Love Not War

Hippie at heart
From the start
    Long haired
    Bell bottomed
    Wide eyed girl
Psychedelic attitude
Dabbler in the esoteric
Beaded bracelet of beliefs
Sprung from ancient philosophies
And new age rituals
On fire for
Life's next experiment
Still wondering how to
Make a world of love
Not war

Finding Myself

I am still finding myself
And not from being lost
Creativity seeping from ossified wounds
Hope reflected in trouble, treachery, turmoil
Awe expanding with each lived day
Joy surging from the smallest of graces
Binding
    Combining
        Renewing
            Deepening
The well is vast

If I Knew Then

If I knew then
    What I know now
I would find you sooner
    Listen deeper
        Learn you are light
I would deafen to inner and outer voices
    Know you are strong
        Kneel in your glow
I would grasp your hand
    Walk you from dark corners
        Ward off your demons
I would take you on adventures
    Run wild with abandon
        Rest full with exhaustion
Let's start now
    Better late than never

Taking It In

Spring dawns in
Life's winter
Sun stretching to
Fill each day
Rays caress
My being
Reminder to
Soak up
Each particle of
    Grace
    Gratitude
    Hope
For once in
My life
I'm taking it
All in

Life Beckons

Life beckons
Like a call to prayer
Fighting all the way
Jumping into a raging storm
Doubts of survival
Fear forms tight bands
Compressing
  Gut
    Heart
      Heart
Pushing against
    Pain
      Grief
        Hopelessness
Wrestling to uncover day's light
Breathing
    Resting until
Life beckons
    Again and again
Unsure life strengthens
Convinced we endure
    Storm after storm

15

Starlight

I was told of the Northern Lights
But never made it far enough north
I wished on stars from my driveway
Yet have no idea what I wished for
I still feel myself standing there
Lost in a sea of vastness
Latching onto pinpricks of hope

Filaments

Filaments of filigree frolicking
As sunbeams bounce off
The crystalline creek
I would not survive if not for
    Sunlight
    Rushing water
    Ice
Reluctant reminders reciting
An evolving poem of life
A poem tumbling off the page
Recombining
    Words
    Thoughts
    Insights
An eternal stew more flavorful
With each turn of the wheel

19

Temple of Trees

Temple of trees
Fanning me with
Breeze of memories
All I know is now
And remnants of then
Sanctuary of sight and sound
Where all that's lost is found
As feet grasp ground

Moon Glow

Moon glow bathing
  Room in honey

Getting stuck
  In sweet memories

Dim lit night
  Shadows playing
    Hide and seek

Branches
  Creaking
    Crackling

Deer and raccoons and skunks
  Frolicking in
    Land rightfully theirs

Drawing me in
  Like a native flute

23

Coaxing

Coaxing colors
From the rainbow
In bold whispers
It can be done
Not without disruption
Order irrelevant
Some colors may bleed
Some colors may blend

Creation

She whispers into consciousness
    Planting an image
        Cultivating a scene
            Flowering into a story
Dropping me in as
    Observer
        Actor
            Dreamer
Spellbound I revisit
Again and again
    Seeking subtle surprises
    Playing piecemeal parts
The muse manifests
Art is born
    Poem
        Drawing
            Song
I the channel

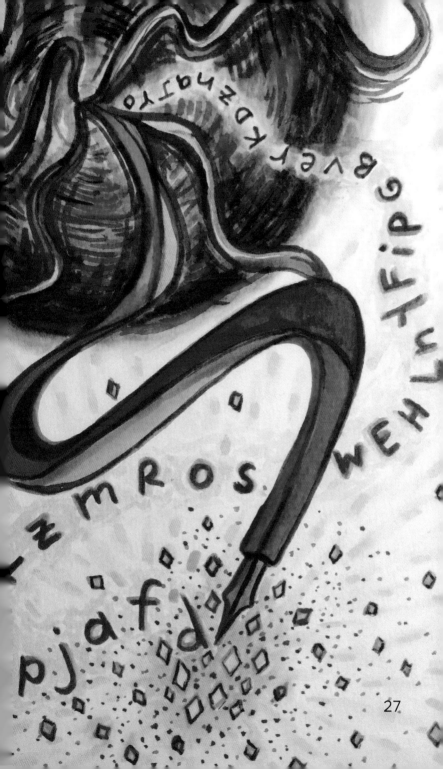

Teamwork

The imposter rises
Nothing new
   Under the sun
   Under the moon
   Under the stars

The alchemist mixes
And remixes
   Words
   Thoughts
   Insights

Together they create
   And recreate
     Ad infinitum

Creativity

From whence chimes
The first note
Who plants the seed
Of the dream
Certainly we don't create
From nothingness
Perhaps an underground pool
Brimming with every
Sound and image
Waits for us
To caste our bucket
Into the void
Combinations endless
Opportunities eternal

Presence

To be in the garden of
Another's presence
Realizing we bask in the
Beauty of the same flowers
And learning of more
Wondrous species often
Hidden in plain site
To tend and nurture
And spread around
Is there any more we
Could wish for?

Tea House

A quaint tea house
Situated on a pebble lot
Paned glass doors
Rough wooden floors
I find myself here often
   Sipping tea
   Reading
   Writing
Connecting with soul friends
We laugh and gaze
Beyond the rims of
Each other's eyes with
Astute recognition
Cinnamon and Jasmine
Imbuing the fragrance of life

Merge

It starts with curiosity
Then a doorway to the soul
Spiraling back and forth
    Attraction
        Attachment
           Empathy
           Love
This yearning to merge

Tapestries

What if I never journeyed
To the hinterland of despair
To meet fellow travelers
Bereft of
    Joy
    Purpose
    Hope
Loss brought me there
Scrambling amidst
Uneven stones
A hollow pitcher seeking
A slow gentle rain
Little filaments of you
Braided with strands of me
Forming a thread of shared history
To weave into our tapestries

39

Merging Worlds

You live in the land of summer
I toe dance among snow
Capped mountain peaks
I dream of thousands of
Cosmos blooms
Showering from the sky
Creating an eternal summer
Amidst the snow

Generosity

Blooming
Anticipating sunlight
Tamped into ground
Forcefully
Carrying
Memory
Inertia
Interest
Terror
Stunned
Searching unknown rooms
Gathering jewels from
Dank corners
Gems are living
Flourishing when
Planted in
Each other
Generosity awakens

Opening Up

Come sit in the
Dust of my home
Walk with me
Through weeds of
  Past
  Present
  Future

Shades up
Windows open

Pride slipping away
Like bark from
An ancient tree

You may see
Someone different
Than you have
Come to know

Then again you
May have seen me
All along
In spite of
My camouflage

Grief

Grief weaves a basket
Around heartbreak
Stretchy and strong

Waxing and waning
Heartbreak's intensity
Tests grief's capacity

Yet grief is limitless
Cradling heartbreak
Like a womb

Nourishing with
   Memories
   Experience
   Hope

Promising
   Rebirth
   Growth
   More heartbreak

Life

Each passing year
The fissure widens
From loss
Loss of people
Loss of time
Loss of facility

Of late I catch
Myself smiling
Surprised
As when a cool breeze
Sneaks up on a torrid day

Awed by the
Gift of life
Amazed by
Life's gifts
Reminded to
Live while alive

Through a Lens Clearly

Leaving the inner world
For perceived necessities
Hurrying back like
A homing pigeon
Is it comfort's allure
Or reality beckoning
Dreaming of walking on air
Through the canopy
Perching in the crook of a tree
Viewing life through
A lens clearly
From a seat of integration
Rather than observation
Wondering about necessities

Lotus Egg

Sitting in lotus pose
Within my heart
Reverberating
Magnificent egg in hand
    Pulsating
    Brightening
    Growing

Pondering its origin
Unaware I have
Given birth
    Fertile
    Creative
    Transforming

Awe evokes terror
What if I am
Consumed by beauty?
Ego is dissolving

Replicating fuchsia droplets
Emerging inward and outward
Orbs of compassion
Perpetual lotus flower
Generating hope

Gather

Gather the tinder from
>Dawn and dusk

>Tears and laughter

>Thoughts and memories

Kindle the spark

Within the heart

Stoke the fire

Consuming
>Fear

>Doubt

>Want

Grow the flame

Ignite the world with love

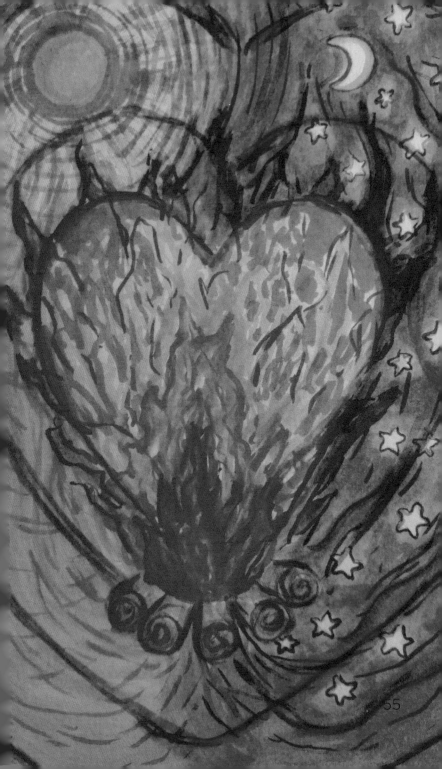

Meet the Poet:

Jackene Laverty

Following a long, satisfying career in healthcare, nutrition and education Jackene now finds fulfillment in expressing herself creatively through poetry.

Jackene and Karen met through a mutual friend, Sunitha Narayanan, during the initial phase of the pandemic. Karen generously hosted online sessions gently coaxing participants to express themselves creatively through doodling.

Jackene Laverty lives in Cincinnati, Ohio with her husband, Tom. They have two adult sons, Justin (Kelsey) and grandson, Graham and Jonathan (Joie).

Meet the Illustrator:

Karen Light

Karen is an artist, a doodler, an illustrator, and a fan of Jackene's poetry! Long before Jackene asked her to illustrate *Gathering*, she spontaneously created doodles inspired by Jackene's beautiful words and is grateful it has turned into this creative collaboration.

Karen's illustrations capture her experience of the poems and are offered as another reflection for the reader to ponder.

Karen lives in Cincinnati, Ohio with her partner, Hector, and their two kitties. She loves to contemplate life's mysteries through art, poetry, dance, and nature.